THE SECRET LIFE
of GIRLFRIENDS

Lenore Skomal

Magnetic Quotes
& Affirmations

Cider Mill Press

ISBN: 1-933662-21-2

This book may be ordered by mail from the publisher.
Please include $4.50 for postage and handling.

Please support your local bookseller first!

Books published by Cider Mill Press Book Publishers are available
at special discounts for bulk purchases in the United States
by corporations, institutions, and other organizations.
For more information, please contact the publisher.

Cider Mill Press Book Publishers
"Where good books are ready for press"
12 Port Farm Road
Kennebunkport, Maine 04046

Visit us on the web!
www.cidermillpress.com

Cover design by: Melany Kuhn
Design by: Mike Rivilis
Typography: Agenda, Mrs. Eaves, Nuptial Script, Type Embellisments One
Printed in China
1 2 3 4 5 6 7 8 9 0
First Edition

Table of Contents

CHAPTER 1:

What Is a Girlfriend?

Now our blood flows through each other as is done for all eternity, loyal forever, we raise our voices in the words of Mumbo Gumbo . . . YA YA!

—Vivi,
Divine Secrets of the Ya-Ya Sisterhood

When the young girls of the Ya-Ya Sisterhood gathered around the fire to pledge their lifelong friendship and devotion to each other, they may not have been aware that the ritual they were innocently enacting actually had a lush history that spans several millennia. The need to create a sister bond with other women is as ancient as the celestial skies, and still very much a part of our culture. For many of us, those bonds run deep, and we are as loyal to our female friends as we are to our own families. Since we have the ability to pick and choose our friends, we have even more reason to love them. Where would you be in your life without your girlfriends? They sustain you, right you, harbor you, laugh with you, and love you.

The special bond between women is as old as civilization itself. Women have always regarded each other not only as touchstones but also as cornerstones for their emotional survival. Sociologists point to the uniqueness and solidarity of that bond being forged, in part, by patriarchal cultures that forced women to be subservient, economically and financially dependent, and devoid of the rights and legal privilege afforded to men.

In short, women-to-women friendships have been fueled historically by desperation and adversity, not to mention companionship, understanding, and compassion.

Women have shared, either publicly or quietly, in rituals like the Ya-Ya Sisterhood throughout history. Blood sisters can be found as far back as the primitive ages. Women sought female kindred spirits for companionship and sisterhood for their emotional survival as much as they sought male companionship for survival of the species.

This ancient bonding of friends is still seen today in ceremonies across the world that draws upon these past rituals.

In Latin America, for instance, a ritual known as *compadrazgo* is still conducted to this day. The ceremony in which friends vow to materially and emotionally support each other for the long-term binds them not just for this lifetime, but for generations. So significant is this ritual that it often involves sharing economic resources and even the raising of each other's children, as well as consecrating emotionally significant friendships. The two friends commit their souls to each other.

In Africa, it is called *kasendi*, which commits friends together in a blood exchange mixed with a drink and denotes that the two individuals are now bound much like blood sisters, committed to each other in a way that supercedes familial and even generational ties. This deep connection means undying loyalty and devotion.

Native Hawaiians also have friendship rituals. One of the more commonly practiced is *pili hoaloha,* which cements a friendship for eternity and involves a ceremony in which friends take vows to commit their undying friendship to each other.

Saheli, Sakhi, Sathin, Bhayeli, and *Hamsheera* are all names that exist as part of the linguistic and cultural code of female friendships in the northern region of India. Women are bonded together in myriad forms of relationships, all of them held sacred and superceding those rituals—such as marriage—that bond women to men.

Such is the intensity of female friendship across the globe. Much more common today in the Western world is what is known as the *friendship commitment ceremony,* which is a

more commonly expressed ritual in which two women are joined together in a lifelong friendship or union by a religious or spiritual ceremony including symbolic elements, prayers, and an exchange of gifts or vows. These ceremonies are becoming more common, especially as we see many women choosing not to marry and have a traditional family. Female friendships are often considered a replacement for that.

All of these rituals basically sanction the woman's right to create a chosen family, namely, a circle of friends who treat each other as family and whose loyalty goes beyond the boundaries of the routine.

Whether you have such a friendship or not isn't really the point. No one is saying you need to go out there, prick your finger, and mix blood with your sisterhood. Rather, the point is that the friendship bonds between women have a secret, sublime nature that often goes beyond verbal description. It is felt.

Oh to be young again! To huddle under a blanket at a slumber party, giggling and hugging, sharing secrets, and just being thrilled about having girlfriends. We learn about the special bond of being a girlfriend at such a young age because many of us live it. We cry and fight over our friendships with each other as if the world was ending. There is such drama and heartfelt emotion wrapped up in every friendship. We long for hours of telephone conversations. We get nervously excited at the prospect of sleeping over at each other's houses. In short, being a friend is more important than just about anything else in a young girl's life. That is, until boys enter the picture.

Seems when the opposite sex comes onto the radar, the innocence and purity of our girl friendships is lost. Boys become the focus, and everything else pales in comparison. And the sad part is, we never can quite regain it, although we spend most of our adult lives trying to.

How often do we plan a girls' night out, spa trips, long luncheons, even longer phone calls—all in the effort to regain or, at the very least, imitate just a small portion of what we've lost? We are desperate for female companionship and intimacy, the cornerstones of what many of us had or perhaps didn't have, but so desperately wanted. We spend our lifetimes trying to rebuild it.

In some ways, female friendships can be the hardest to maintain. They require much of us internally, including the ability to rise over our pettiness, our insecurities, our innate selfishness, our fear of commitment, and our natural protective instincts of home and family. It means placing a priority on relationships over sometimes pressing daily issues, over our partnerships with members of the opposite sex, over our own laziness, and sometimes over our families. But the payback is well worth it.

In short, the best of us as women lies in our ability to be true and abiding friends to one another.

CHAPTER 2:
The Art of Friendship

When asked what is a friend,
Taoist philosopher Chuang Tzu responded
with a question. "Who can live together without
any special effort to live together and help
each other without any special effort to help
each other?" The answer: a true friend.

Friendships should be effortless. Ideally they should be easy, happy relationships you fall into like a cool lake on a hot, airless day, or wrap around you like a blanket in front of a flaming fire on a bitter night. They should be comforting, fun, and inviting, unfettered by lesser emotions like jealousy, insecurity, and selfishness. They should be simpler than relationships with men because of the mutual understanding of our sisterhood. They should be more complete because of the circle of women to which we all belong. There should be none of the miscommunication that comes with relationships with the opposite sex because the desperate desire to be understood is no longer a problem. It is . . . well . . . understood.

There are many types of female friendships. Aristotle divided them into three categories: friendships for usefulness, friendships for pleasure, and friendships of virtue. Do with that what you will. It is simpler to divide them into more useful categories such as acquaintances, work friends, social friends, good friends, and best friends, or what you might call *heart sisters*. While the others are self-explanatory, heart sisters are those girlfriends whom you feel bonded to by a deep, spiritual connection. No matter what happens, you can always pick up where you left off, never missing a beat. There is a heart connection between them, almost as if they were real blood sisters to you. Much never needs to be said between you and your heart sisters. They are your biggest fans, constant supporters, and the ones who truly believe you can do no wrong. They love you unconditionally, love to hang out with you, and will rush to your side if you are in pain. Oftentimes, they know something isn't quite right just by the sound of your voice. If you have one of these friendships, you are blessed.

While not all of our friends can be categorized as heart sisters or best friends, each one of our friends serves a function in our lives. It's like having a whole bunch of shoes or outfits in your closet. You need a variety to fit different needs and situations. It's great if you have a one-size-fits-all friend. There is nothing wrong with wearing the same outfit every day, but sometimes it is just not appropriate. Equally, there is nothing wrong with having a variety of different friends, who have very different personalities and interests. Ultimately, they are a reflection of you and your varied needs and personalities.

Having friends not only improves your health, it can actually help you live longer. There is a healing power to friendship that shouldn't be overlooked.

In stressful times, as women, we're more inclined to seek out friends. That social support can lower our blood pressure, which signals our adrenal glands to stop pumping out corticosteroids and that acts as a stress reducer. As a result of spending time with a girlfriend, we feel less anxious, less overwrought, less overwhelmed. And our bodies reflect that. We may even live longer as a result of coping this way. And this friendship response to stress may also explain why women outlive men.

Friend is an Anglo-Saxon word that was originally derived from a verb form meaning, literally, *beloved*, or *one who is loving*. That quality of loving is central to an abiding friendship. A great friendship is one in which love, and all the respect, honor, and truth that come along with it, is center stage. These are the most important points:

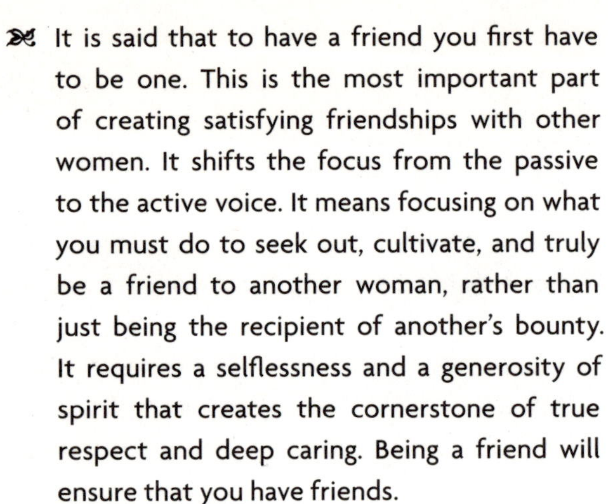

✍ It is said that to have a friend you first have to be one. This is the most important part of creating satisfying friendships with other women. It shifts the focus from the passive to the active voice. It means focusing on what you must do to seek out, cultivate, and truly be a friend to another woman, rather than just being the recipient of another's bounty. It requires a selflessness and a generosity of spirit that creates the cornerstone of true respect and deep caring. Being a friend will ensure that you have friends.

✍ Friendships need to be cared for. And that is the secret to them. The truth is that actively maintaining girl-to-girl friendships gets harder the older we get. Be active in your friendships. Take care of them. Water, cultivate, and tend to them. Make time for your friendships. Your problems will always be there, but your friends might not.

At the heart of it, sterling friendship is really a matter of offering a nonjudgmental bond to those we cherish. Toast your friends for always bringing out the best in you . . . and the worst. It's the secret of female friendships. We have a happy way of creating a safe place for each other—a place where we can cry, act silly, rant, and most of all, laugh. Laughter is a wonderful by-product of a good friendship. Love your friends for giving this respite from what can be sometimes an overwhelming, overburdening life. The older you get, perhaps this will be what you become most grateful

for . . . being able to laugh, let your hair down, feel loved, and most of all, be understood by those who accept you for who you are and wouldn't change a thing.

❧ In good times and in bad, for better or for worse, that should be the unspoken vow among girlfriends. A true friend offers you what you need, even if you don't know it. Whether it be dragging you out to socialize when you want nothing more than to stay inside and curl yourself around your pain. Or forcing you to talk about something you would rather ignore. Or telling you how great you look on your worst hair day ever. That's true friendship. Don't we want friends who are willing to lie to us just to make us feel better? That's what real girlfriends do. We

bolster each other up, even if we risk going to hell to do so.

For some, being a friend to another woman does not come easily. It's not uncommon to hear, "Most of my friends are men. Women just don't like me." They sound as if they are proud of that— as if aligning themselves with men and creating only male friendships is a badge of honor. The message they want you to believe is that only unique women can hang with men. But quite the opposite is true. Hanging with men is easy. It requires no personal ante, no risk, no measure of effort. You just have to show up.

With women, the more honest you can be and the more risk you are willing to take, the more you will be rewarded. You have to come to the party willing to strip away something of yourself—willing to be truly you. The more you can risk showing your true self, the more you will be able to deepen the relationships that are there. You need to be real.

We are sisters, friends, bonded by our gender and so much more. Don't miss out on the party. Come celebrate.

CHAPTER 3:
Saying Good-bye

The endings always come too fast.
They come too fast and they pass too slow.

——Simon & Garfunkel

It is the innate nature of some friendships to end. Choice or chance—there is debate over which is emotionally harder or more excruciating to navigate.

Endings are always awkward and uncomfortable. That's why many of us don't officially end our friendships. We're cowards. Or perhaps we just don't want to hurt anyone's feelings. So like bad boyfriends, we just stop calling. Or returning phone calls. After all, neglect is the best weapon to kill a dying friendship.

Friendships end for a variety of reasons—all of them are universal but still as unique as the two women involved. I have walked away from many friendships in my life. And many of my friends have walked away from me. It is never easy.

These are not friendships that dwindle over time because of maturity, geography, negligence, or lack of interest. These are friendships that are active, ongoing, living, breathing things; relationships that for some reason have reached a point where you feel compelled to make a decision. The truth is, either you make it or someone else will.

ALL ABOUT ME

But enough about me, let's talk about you. What do YOU think of me?

—CC Bloom, *Beaches*

Some friendships are just doomed from the start. A lack of boundaries is often the precursor to friendships doomed to fail, for instance, when your friend is much more preoccupied with herself, suffering from a chronic case of me-ism, which over time repeatedly takes precedence over caring about you and your problems. You find yourself swallowing bits of yourself, stifling your personal need to share your joys and sufferings, and being forced to cater to the whims of your self-absorbed friend.

It is not only tiresome and unfair; it can feel hurtful and selfish.

Undoubtedly, making the decision to let go of a friend who has become an emotional burden can be one of the most freeing experiences. But it can be riddled with feelings of guilt and a sense of failure. Most women do not like to cut off friendships, even if they are lopsided. We struggle with trying to make them work, even if they are no longer satisfying to us. Selfish friends are truly no friends at all. They tend to put their own needs center stage and find it hard to truly share in your troubles or joys.

When it's time to end the relationship, oftentimes shifting gears to talking only about yourself and never asking about her can hasten the demise.

Bored with having to listen to you talk about you, these friends frequently go away on their own.

The lesson learned here is that at the very basic level, friendships have to be two-way—mutual give and take in order to be functional and healthy. If they aren't, then you are staying in them for the wrong reason.

BRICK WALL

Suffering is overrated.

—Bill Veeck

Ever have a friend who mulls the same problem over and over and over again? You find yourself giving the same advice, being summarily placated and then ignored. It's frustrating, and when you begin to see the pattern, you get pretty disgusted. Am I beating my head against a brick wall?

It is true that some people just like to be miserable. They really don't want help with their problems, because somehow they define themselves by their problems. To be understood and commiserated with is their goal. They cling to their victimization like it is the only thing that is truly theirs.

When someone like this is in your life, you have options. You can stay in the friendship, be the person to whom she reiterates her state in life time and time again, and shrug it off as you always do.

Or you can move on.

Personally, this type of friend can drive you crazy. And the older you get, the more valuable your time is. These types of friends require a lot of energy to deal with. If there is a deeper bond that keeps you together, then suck it up and stay with it. If there isn't, then go to the next step. Try to right this unbalanced relationship. If after several attempts this isn't possible, let the relationship slide. These friendships can be a blatant disregard for your feelings and a waste of time and energy. You are not merely a warm body or a sounding board. If you are, then there is nothing unique about you.

She can find any number of people to whine to. So why not let her?

THE GREEN-EYED MONSTER

I was jealous. I was so jealous of you I couldn't see straight! You did everything you said you were going to do, everything! And your talent, this incredible talent! I can't even yodel!

—Hillary Essex, *Beaches*

The truth of the matter is that one of the reasons there is a secret language of girlfriends is because we have to overcome so much of our own negative nature to create it. And when you have to work that hard, you find that you have created something much greater than the sum total of two people. And that can be wonderful. Being happy for each other's accomplishments, joys, and sweet successes is a truly freeing experience.

But some girlfriends never can quite get there. To overcome their own pettiness is a constant struggle. It's easy to forgive that frailty, especially if the relationship has true depth and commitment.

But sometimes jealousy can destroy a friendship at its very roots.

We all know at least one friend who has this problem—and maybe it is us. That niggling jealousy just rears its head when another has a stroke of good fortune. Our tendency may be to downplay our own success to compensate for this flaw. But this can be tedious. And, ultimately, it is difficult to do. How can you be true to yourself if you can't enjoy your successes with your friend? Always having to be careful to downplay those successes is unhealthy.

Jealousy stems from insecurity. There's not much you can do to help someone who is chronically insecure enough to get upset about the good things that happen in your life. At some point it will come to a crossroads, and you will have to decide whether swallowing your happiness is worth it.

FORK IN THE ROAD

No person is your friend who demands your silence, or denies your right to grow and be perceived as fully blossomed as you were intended.

—Alice Walker

Usually, when long-term relationships end, it is a long time in the making. Old friendships don't just end. The women involved in them make a decision to end them. Making that conscious decision to say good-bye to a longtime friend is perhaps one of the most painful decisions in the world. Often it comes after arduous personal, internal debate, which sometimes can last years.

Complex in nature, long-term friendships that end often have the seeds of unresolved problems early on. If they are not resolved, they can bloom into trees with very complex root systems. Grow they will until there is usually one defining moment, episode, argument, or misunderstanding that blows the relationship apart. Both parties know that it has been a long time coming.

What drives old friends to finally break ties? In some instances it involves a test of your own personal convictions and integrity, challenging you to make a choice: your values versus your friendship. It can involve behaviors—often self-destructive in nature—that have an incredibly adverse affect not only on your friend but on you and the relationship as well.

While a sterling quality in a friend is being unconditionally accepting and nonjudgmental, it doesn't mean that you have to turn your back on what you hold in most esteem—your sense of moral right and wrong. It can be hard to find the line between total unconditional love and being played for a fool.

The question you must ask yourself is this: Can I turn a blind eye to that to which I would never turn a blind eye in anyone else, even myself? What you have to weigh is what personal cost you are willing to pay to keep this friendship. Remember, no one is saved unless she wants to be. Perhaps it's time to stop trying.

No one wants to walk away from a long-term friendship. But like a bad marriage, maintaining a self-destructive friendship purely because of "time logged in" is not reason enough to stay.

ENTER DEATH

Love is something eternal. The aspect may change, but not the love.

—Vincent Van Gogh

When fate plays a hand and takes your friend away, it can be even harder on you than deciding to deliberately cut ties. What you need to know is that death doesn't take your friendships away, it just transforms them. That can be a tough leap.

The grief that follows the death of a dear friend is exquisite—sharp, all encompassing, and, sadly, long-term. It can be said that losing a friend is like cutting a thick electric cable that is filled with thousands of tiny colored wires. While the enormity of the loss felt at the beginning can be likened to the initial slice of the cable, it's only as time goes on that we start to feel the loss of each thin wire. Those wires represent the many ways we are connected to a loved friend. We may suddenly rush to the phone to share a particularly juicy bit of gossip, only to remember that she is no longer on the other end. Another wire cut. Or, we happily anticipate an upcoming birthday, only to realize, with despair, there are no more

birthdays being celebrated—only the anniversaries of her death. Yet another wire gone.

But as much as the gnawing ache of loss leaves a hole in your life, it also signals something else—a transformation of that relationship into something much more spiritual, one that does not rely on the physical world, but on the unseen one. Those friendships live on, just not in the way that we are used to. Our friends guide us, comfort us, protect us, and even offer us amazing opportunities to know them as they are now—but we need to listen. Change does not come easy to any woman. But if we can learn change and open our lives to the possibility that they are still with us, you would be amazed at what you find. Talk to your friend, wherever she may be. Ask for her help; send her your love and listen with your heart

and senses for her reply. It may come in the whiff of a cigarette when no one is smoking, a special song on the radio that you associate with her, a signature phrase that she used to say coming out of the mouth of someone else. She is still with you. Never doubt that.

CHAPTER 4:

Quotes

1. *Lots of people want to ride with you in the limo, but what you want is someone who will take the bus with you when the limo breaks down.*

—Oprah Winfrey

2. *A true friend is someone who thinks that you are a good egg, even though he knows that you are slightly cracked.*

—Bernard Meltzer

3. *Good friends must not always be together; it is the feeling of oneness when distant that proves a lasting friendship.*

—Susan P. Schultz

4. *Each friend represents a world in us, a world possibly not born until they arrive, and it is only by this meeting that a new world is born.*

—Anais Nin

5. *Love is blind, but friendship closes its eyes.*

—Unknown

6. *Don't walk in front of me, I may not follow / Don't walk behind me, I may not lead / Just walk beside me and be my friend.*

—Unknown

7. *I do not want a friend / Who smiles when I smile / Who weeps when I weep / For my shadow in the pool / Can do better than that.*

—Confucious

8. *A friend is a gift you give yourself.*

—Robert Louis Stevenson

9. *Odd how much it hurts when a friend moves away——and leaves behind only silence.*

—Pam Brown

10. *To know someone here or there with whom you can feel there is understanding in spite of distances or thoughts expressed. That can make life a garden.*

—Goethe

11. *My best friend is the one that brings out the best in me.*

—Henry Ford

12. *Friends are God's way of apologizing to us for our families.*

—Unknown

13. *A friend is one who knows all about you and likes you anyway.*

—Christi Mary Warner

14. *The most I can do for my friend is simply to be his friend.*

—Henry David Thoreau

15. *My best friend is the man who in wishing me well wishes it for my sake.*

—Aristotle

16. *It is one of the blessings of old friends that you can afford to be stupid with them.*

—Ralph Waldo Emerson

17. *However rare true love may be, it is less so than true friendship.*

—François Duc de la Rochefoucauld

18. *Hold a true friend with both your hands.*

—Nigerian Proverb

19. *To me, fair friend, you never can be old / For as you were when first your eye I eyed, / Such seems your beauty still.*

—William Shakespeare

20. *Love demands infinitely less than friendship.*

—George Jean Nathan

21. *It's no good trying to keep up old friendships. It's painful for both sides. The fact is, one grows out of people, and the only thing is to face it.*

—W. Somerset Maugham

22. *The proper office of a friend is to side with you when you are in the wrong. Nearly anybody will side with you when you are in the right.*

—Mark Twain

23. *You can hardly make a friend in a year, but you can easily offend one in an hour.*

—Chinese Proverb

24. *We are all travelers in the wilderness of this world, and the best we can find in our travels is an honest friend.*

—Robert Lewis Stevenson

25. *Nine-tenths of the people were created so you would want to be with the other tenth.*

—Horace Walpole

26. *Friendship is born at the moment when one person says to another, "What? You too? I thought I was the only one."*

—C. S. Lewis

27. *The difference between friendship and love is how much you can hurt each other.*

—Ashleigh Brilliant

28. *An old friend will help you move. A good friend will help you move a dead body.*

—Jim Hayes

29. *A good reason to only maintain a small circle of friends is that three out of four murders are committed by people who know the victim.*

—George Carlin

30. *Friendship is the only cement that will ever hold the world together.*

—Woodrow Wilson

31. *Long, long afterward, in an oak / I found the arrow, still unbroke; / And the song, from beginning to end, / I found again in the heart of a friend.*

—Henry Wadsworth Longfellow

32. *Friendship multiplies the good of life and divides the evil.*

—Baltasar Gracian

33. *A real friend is someone who walks in when the rest of the world walks out.*

—Proverb

34. *No distance of place or lapse of time can lessen the friendship of those who are thoroughly persuaded of each other's worth.*

—Robert Southey

35. *The road to a friend's house is never too long.*

—Danish Proverb

36. *The ideal friendship is to feel as one while remaining two.*

—Anne Sophie Swetchine

37. *If all my friends were to jump off a bridge, I wouldn't jump with them. I'd be at the bottom to catch them.*

—Unknown

38. *The greatest sweetener of human life is Friendship. To raise this to the highest pitch of enjoyment, is a secret which but few discover.*

—Joseph Addison

39. *A friend drops their plans when you're in trouble, shares joy in your accomplishments, feels sad when you're in pain. A friend encourages your dreams and offers advice-- but when you don't follow it, they still respect and love you.*

—Doris Wild Helmering

40. *Choose your friends carefully. Your enemies will choose you.*

—Yasser Arafat

41. *Little friends may prove great friends.*

—Aesop

42. *We cannot do great things. We can only do little things with great love.*

—Mother Teresa

43. *Friends are those rare people who ask how we are and then wait to hear the answer.*

—Ed Cunningham

44. *A friend is someone who, upon seeing another friend in immense pain, would rather be the one experiencing the pain, than to have to watch their friend suffer.*

—Amanda Gier

45. *A friend to everybody and to nobody is the same thing.*

—Spanish Proverb

46. *It takes a long time to grow an old friend.*

—John Leonard

47. *When we honestly ask ourselves which person in our lives means the most to us, we often find that it is those who, instead of giving advice, solutions, or cures, have chosen rather to share our pain and touch our wounds with a warm and tender hand. The friend who can be silent with us in a moment of despair or confusion, who can stay with us in an hour of grief and bereavement, who can tolerate not knowing, not curing, not healing and face with us the reality of our powerlessness, that is a friend who cares.*

—Henri Nouwen

48. *In my friend, I find a second self.*

—Isabel Norton

49. *False friends are worst than bitter enemies.*

—Scottish Proverb

50. *Our friends should be companions who inspire us, who help us rise to our best.*

—Joseph B. Wirthlin

51. *When a virtuous man is raised, it brings gladness to his friends, grief to his enemies, and glory to his posterity.*

—Ben Jonson

52. *Friendship never explains—your friends do not need it, and your enemies will not believe it anyway. A real friend never gets in your way, unless you happen to be on the way down. A friend is someone you can do nothing with and enjoy it. However much we guard ourselves against it, we tend to shape ourselves in the image others have of us. It is not so much the example of others we imitate, as the reflection of ourselves in their eyes and the echo of ourselves in their words.*

—Eric Hoffer

53. *A friend is someone who reaches for your hand but touches your heart.*

—Kathleen Grove

54. *A friend is a person who knows what you are saying even if you're not talking.*

—Sarah Bennett

55. *The friendship isn't worth the tears unless the friend is.*

—Kellina Filbin

56. *Trouble is a sieve through which we sift our acquaintances. Those too big to pass through are our friends.*

—Arlene Francis

57. *The best part of life is when your family becomes your friends and your friends become your family.*

—Danica Whitefield

58. *A real friend is one who walks in when the rest of the world walks out.*

—Walter Winchell

59. *The most beautiful discovery that true friends can make is that they can grow separately without growing apart.*

—Elizabeth Foley

60. *A best friend never stops believing in you, even if you give up on yourself.*

—Renee Duvall

CHAPTER 5:
31 Insights and Affirmations

1. *Friends are like stars. You don't always see them but you know they are there.*

—Hulali Luta

Strong female relationships have one thing in common—consistency. They are as constant as stars above. *I greet my friends with love and enthusiasm, thankful for their existence in my life.*

2. *Lost and found.*

It's time to find your long-lost friend. You know, the one that you've been meaning to find over the last few years, but just haven't taken the time to do so. Don't let another day go by without trying. *Today I will find my lost friend.*

3. *Treat your friends as you do your pictures. Place them in the best light.*

—Jennie Jerome Churchill

Hold each other in high esteem and honor. If you can glorify your dear friends and focus on their good qualities and their strengths, it will help you be less harsh with yourself. *I will find uniqueness in each friend and herald it.*

4. *Let her know she is heard.*

Yeah, I called her up. She gave me a bunch of crap about me not listening to her, or something. I don't know. I wasn't really paying attention.

—Harry, *Dumb & Dumber*

Do you know someone who has an unresponsive mate? Today is the day to take some time to give her a call, and let her bend your ear. *I have two ears to listen, two shoulders to be cried upon, and I will give them freely today to a friend.*

5. *A friend knows the song in my heart and sings it to me when my memory fails.*

—Donna Roberts

When you lose your way, a true friend helps you find it. She reminds you of where you are going. *I will let my friends love me and compliment me, and I will let myself feel good about that.*

6. *Lighten her load.*

You most likely have a girlfriend, close friend, or acquaintance who is completely overwhelmed in her life. Today is the day you help her. You might never know just how much it means, but remember, everything is recorded in the universe.

7. *A true friend is there for you when they would rather be someplace else.*

—Unknown

Selflessness is a wonderful quality of friendship. But it is hard to remember what a friend is sacrificing in order to support you. *I will take special notice of my friends and their generosity and deeply thank them for it.*

8. *As time goes by.*
Life has a way of pushing some friends onto the back burner. And while guilt is a wonderful motivator—you have to act on it for it to be effective. *I choose not to neglect my friends.*

9. *Everyone hears what you say. Friends listen to what you say. Best friends listen to what you don't say.*

—Unknown

Intuition between friends is the unspoken language that binds. Knowing each other well enough to understand what is not being said is the secret language of friendship. *I trust my instincts and will act on them with my friends.*

10. *Learn forgiveness for others.*

Only you know if you have been unduly harsh or judgmental with a friend. Maybe it's time to forgive her. *Forgiveness will take the weight off my soul. I am tired of being angry and hurt.*

11. *A friend can tell you things you don't want to tell yourself.*

—Frances Ward Weller

In the end, it's all about honesty. No one wants a false friend, a phony, a liar, or a kiss-up. While we seek sincerity from our girlfriends, we also don't want someone who is judgmental. *I trust that my friends will tell me what I need to hear.*

12. *Don't forget the red tent.*
Writer Anita Diamant takes us back to biblical times, when the red tent was a place for women to live when they were having a baby or a period. Create a red tent for your best friends. *I will bond in the way that underscores my sisterhood with these women.*

13. *Since there is nothing so well worth having as friends, never lose a chance to make them.*
—Francesco Guicciardini
Always be open to new friendships. It is so much easier and healthier to go through life looking at strangers with grace as opposed to apathy or hostility. *I can make friends easily. People genuinely enjoy my company.*

14. *Extend the red tent to faraway good friends.* Making your friendships a priority extends to your old pals from college, your friends from childhood, your sisters, whomever you hold near and dear. Make it a priority. Start planning today. *I will create a special space for my true friends and myself.*

15. *Often we have no time for our friends but all the time in the world for our enemies.*

—Leon Uris

Be vigilant over what takes up space in your mind and your heart, which often is worry or concern or responsibility that we have attached too much importance to. Reprioritize your thinking. *Say yes to your friends first.*

16. *Special gift giving.*

A nice break from the regular birthday routine is to celebrate in style. Instead of buying separate gifts, friends should throw all their money together and purchase the birthday girl something she really wants and may never buy herself. Remember: *Friendship has no price tag.*

17. *Do not use a hatchet to remove a fly from your friend's forehead.*

—Chinese Proverb

Ask yourself three simple questions before criticizing a friend. What is there to gain by her knowing this? Is it crucial to her happiness? What will be the fallout afterward, and I am prepared to handle it? *Think before I speak.*

18. *Let go of a friendship that has ended.*
Ritual has its place in the loss of friendships, too. Put closure to the act by creating a ritual to say good-bye. Honor that person for what she brought to your life, both the good and the not so good. *Saying good-bye isn't bad—it is just a form of letting go.*

19. *E-friendship.*
There are an abundance of fun and free e-greeting-card companies at your fingertips. It takes seconds to send an e-card. There is so much you can do in five minutes to let a special friend know she is cared for. *It is the small things in life that count most.*

20. *A goddess day.*

A little pampering goes a long way. Set aside time for appointments for your girlfriend and yourself for a manicure, pedicure, or facial. For that hour or two, you don't have to do anything. *I will take time to rest and reflect.*

21. *It's the ones you can call up at 4:00 A.M. that really matter.*

—Marlena Dietrich

How many friends do you have that you can put to the test? How many can put you to that test? Would that call be met with anger or love? *I am here for my friends 24–7.*

22. *Strangers are just friends we have yet to meet.* Embrace the day with the belief that you are part of the larger sum. There are kindred spirits everywhere; you just need to be open to them. *I am open to everyone I meet today as a potential new friend.*

23. *The best mirror of all is an old friend.*

—George Herbert

Among the sterling qualities of an old friendship is the ability to look at an old friend and see the length and breadth of where you came from. How much you have grown, shifted, sweetened, and matured. *Treasure old relationships and treat them with care.*

24. *Love letters.*

Now that most of what we receive in the mail has been reduced to bills and junk, it is wonderful to find a card or letter tucked away in the pile. Next time you are at the grocery store, buy a pack of note cards and write to a friend. *No energy spent is wasted. It all comes back to me.*

25. *The statistics on sanity are that one out of every four Americans is suffering from some sort of mental illness. Think of your three best friends. If they're okay, then it's you.*

—Rita Mae Brown

You have got to laugh at yourself, allow yourself to go a little bit crazy, and be the butt of a good joke. Trust your friends to let you do this. *Let yourself go and trust your friends.*

26. *Create a ritual*

It doesn't have to be something rife with blood oaths or vows. But rituals do create tradition in friendships. Building a routine into your friendships that you can all rely on is a meaningful way to honor your ties. *We are bound together as friends and sisters.*

27. *Forgive yourself.*

You can't be a true friend to others, in every sense of the word, unless you love yourself. That means forgiving yourself if you have guilt over the past. It is over. The present is all we have, and that is very powerful. *I bear no ill will against myself. I am forgiven.*

28. *Be a friend to yourself first.*

Don't expect so much from yourself. If you do, that carries over in other relationships. What can you do for yourself that you would normally do for another? Affirm yourself. *I love and accept myself exactly as I am.*

29. *Buy a birthday book.*

The older we get, the easier we forget. The best present I ever got was a birthday/special occasion book. It is filled with blank pages. No days of the week, just dates. You can fill in the birthdays. *I will plan to lessen my angst.*

30. *Be a good friend.*

Rather than look at yourself as having friends, look at yourself as being a friend. For today, don't wait to be invited somewhere by a friend, you do the inviting. *I am interested in my friends and will take an active role in showing that.*

31. *Go out on a limb. That's where all the fruit is.*

—Will Rogers

To be a good friend, you have to risk something of yourself. What if we were to be bolder? Jump right in and take a chance, and even risk one of our friends being taken aback. *Today, I will take more chances in my friendships.*

About Cider Mill Press Book Publishers

Good ideas ripen with time. From seed to harvest, Cider Mill Press strives to bring fine reading, information, and entertainment together between the covers of its creatively crafted books. Our Cider Mill bears fruit twice a year, publishing a new crop of titles each Spring and Fall.

Visit us on the web at
www.cidermillpress.com
or write to us at
12 Port Farm Road
Kennebunkport, Maine 04046

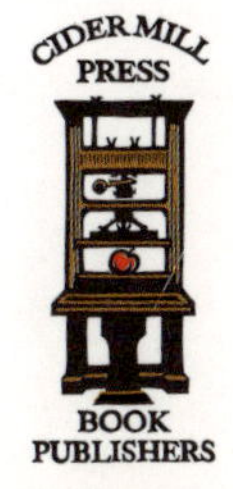

Where Good Books are
Ready for Press